To obtain permission(s) to use the material from this work for any purpose including workshops or seminars, please submit a written request to:

XAMonline, Inc.
25 First Street, Suite 106
Cambridge, MA 02141
Toll Free: 1-800-509-4128
Email: info@xamonline.com
Web: www.xamonline.com
Fax: 1-617-583-5552

Library of Congress Cataloging-in-Publication Data

Wynne, Sharon A.
    ICTS Basic Skills Practice Test 1: Teacher Certification / Sharon A. Wynne. -1st ed.
    ISBN: 978-1-60787-199-6
    1. ICTS Basic Skills Practice Test 1
    2. Study Guides   3. ICTS   4. Teachers' Certification & Licensure
    5. Careers

Disclaimer:

The opinions expressed in this publication are the sole works of XAMonline and were created independently from the National Education Association, Educational Testing Service, or any State Department of Education, National Evaluation Systems or other testing affiliates.

Between the time of publication and printing, state specific standards as well as testing formats and website information may change that is not included in part or in whole within this product. Sample test questions are developed by XAMonline and reflect similar content as on real tests; however, they are not former tests. XAMonline assembles content that aligns with state standards but makes no claims nor guarantees teacher candidates a passing score. Numerical scores are determined by testing companies such as NES or ETS and then are compared with individual state standards. A passing score varies from state to state.

Printed in the United States of America   œ-1

ICTS Basic Skills Practice Test 1
ISBN: 978-1-60787-199-6

READING

Directions: Read the following passage and answer question 1–8.

The Eiffel Tower in Paris, France, is probably the country's most recognizable symbol. Not only is the tower an obvious symbol, but it is also an incredible work of art that was designed by Gustave Eiffel. The tower, which was opened March 31, 1889, was originally built for the Universal Exhibition and was only meant to stand for twenty years then be destroyed. Luckily, the tower still stands to this day in the original post it was constructed.

Between 1889 when the tower opened and December 31, 2008, 243,376,000 people have visited the 324-meter, iron tower. In order to ride to the second floor of the tower, a visitor must pay 8 francs to ride the elevator. To ride all the way to the top floor, a visitor must pay 13 francs. For only 4.50 francs, a visitor can take the stairs. Unfortunately, guests must climb 115 meters to reach the second floor, and stairs are not available for visitors who wish to go to the top of the tower. In other words, visitors who wish to go all the way to the top of the tower must take the elevator.

1. **What is the main idea of the passage?**
   (Average)

   A. The Eiffel Tower opened on March 31, 1889

   B. Many people have visited the Eiffel Tower since it opened

   C. Visitors can take the elevator or the stairs to reach the top of the tower

   D. The Eiffel Tower is a well-known symbol around the world

2. **Why did the author write this article?**
   (Average)

   A. To entertain

   B. To persuade

   C. To describe

   D. To inform

BASIC SKILLS

3. **What is the best summary of the second paragraph?**
   (Rigorous)

   A. Visitors can ride an elevator or take the stairs to reach certain heights of the Eiffel Tower

   B. The Eiffel Tower is very tall and stands 324 meters high

   C. The elevator at the Eiffel Tower only reaches 115 meters

   D. Visitors must pay in order to climb to the top of the Eiffel Tower.

4. **How is the passage above organized?**
   (Average)

   A. Cause and effect

   B. Compare and contrast

   C. Statement support

   D. Sequence of events

5. **What comparison is made in the first paragraph?**
   (Rigorous)

   A. The Eiffel Tower is in Paris, France but is enjoyed by the world

   B. The Eiffel Tower opened in 1889 and is still in the same spot today

   C. The Eiffel Tower is recognizable and it serves as a country's symbol

   D. The Eiffel Tower is a great symbol of France and a work of art

6. **By using the word *luckily* in the final sentence of the first paragraph, what is the author implying?**
   (Rigorous)

   A. That tearing the tower down as originally intended would have been a bad decision

   B. It is a good thing for France that the tower remains in the same spot it was built

   C. If the tower had been torn down, Gustave, its designer would have been angry

   D. The Universal Exhibition can now take place in the exact same spot someday since the tower remains

7. **What words does the author use in paragraph 2 to clarify information for the reader?**
    (Average)

    A. Between

    B. In order to

    C. Unfortunately

    D. In other words

8. **What would have been the best transition word for the author to use to connect these two sentences?**
    (Easy)

    In order to ride to the second floor of the tower, a visitor must pay 8 francs to ride the elevator. To ride all the way to the top floor, a visitor must pay 13 francs.

    A. Next,

    B. Beyond,

    C. For example,

    D. Consequently,

9. **What does the word *pang* mean in the sentence below?**
    (Easy)

    Standing outside of her homeroom, Lauren watched other children enter the room and overheard them sharing stories about their summer adventures. She couldn't help but feel a pang of loneliness as she thought of her best friend Morgan back in Colorado.

    A. Pain

    B. Hint

    C. Depression

    D. Song

10. **What does the word *convoluted* mean in the sentence below?**
    (Easy)

    Misty listened to Marty intently. But as Marty revealed more of her plan, Misty wasn't sure she wanted anything to do with it. Marty's plan was convoluted and twisted and, quite frankly, Misty was worried about her own safety.

    A. Strange

    B. Straight

    C. Thorough

    D. Polluted

11. The book *The Giver* by Lois Lowry is a great book. The characters are interesting and they are unique. Everyone who reads *The Giver* will enjoy it and not be able to put it down.

Is this a valid or invalid argument?
(Average)

A. Valid

B. Invalid

12. I-95 is the best route to take from Virginia to Washington, DC. There are many rest stops along the way so it is easy to stop and get gas, food, and use the restrooms when necessary. There is also an HOV lane that allows those traveling with others to bypass single traveler cars.

Is this a valid or invalid argument?
(Average)

A. Valid

B. Invalid

13. Which sentence in the passage below is irrelevant?
(Rigorous)

Cats was one of the longest running musicals. It opened October 7, 1982, at the Winter Garden Theater in New York City. New York City is also known as Manhattan. The music, which has become very popular and well-known, was written by Andrew Lloyd Webber. He grew up in London, England. Perhaps the best-known hit was "Memory," which became popular worldwide, and was recorded in more than twelve languages. The actual story is based on the book *Old Possum's Book of Practical Cats* written by T.S. Eliot, which is a series of children's poems.

A. *Cats* was one of the longest running musicals.

B. it opened October 7, 1982 at the Winter Garden Theater

C. New York City is also known as Manhattan

D. The music is popular and well-known and was written by Andrew Lloyd Webber

14. **Which sentence in the passage above is irrelevant?**
(Rigorous)

   A. The music, which has become very popular and well-known, was written by Andrew Lloyd Webber.

   B. He grew up in London, England.

   C. Perhaps the best-known hit was "Memory" which became popular worldwide.

   D. The actual story is based on the book, *Old Possum's Book of Practical Cats.*

15. **Elementary school is better than middle school. Is this sentence a fact or an opinion?**
(Easy)

   A. Fact

   B. Opinion

16. **Letter grades are given at Thomas Jefferson Middle School. Is this sentence a fact or an opinion?**
(Easy)

   A. Fact

   B. Opinion

17. **The science fair will take place at 4:00 on Saturday, March 13. Is this sentence a fact or an opinion?**
(Easy)

   A. Fact

   B. Opinion

18. **The science fair will be a lot of fun so everyone should attend. Is this sentence a fact or an opinion?**
(Easy)

   A. Fact

   B. Opinion

19. *Thank you so much for the gift you sent for my birthday. It was nice of you to send me a gift and remember that my birthday was last week. Your generosity is appreciated. Thanks again.*

   John

   What conclusion can be drawn from the above letter?
(Rigorous)

   A. The author and the gift giver are related

   B. The author is a child that received a gift

   C. The gift was a toy and the author liked it

   D. The author didn't really like the gift

20. *Even after turning the lock correctly it still wouldn't open. My combination is 32-41-12; I hope this will help you get to the bottom of the problem. All of my school supplies are locked inside, and I must have them in order to be successful in my classes.*

What conclusion can be drawn from the paragraph above?
(Average)

A. A teacher's belongings are locked inside of her car

B. A student is having trouble with their locker

C. A student's gym locker is jammed

D. A traveler's locker is jammed

Directions: Read the following passage and answer questions 21–24.

It is not news to anyone who has been following the changes in the economy that people are spending less. This is a wise decision by all consumers and since people are reevaluating their spending, it is necessary for companies to reevaluate their plans for growth. Many companies that were spending money on security have had to shift their focus elsewhere. A number of companies have made the decision to focus on virtualization—when one computer completes the jobs of many. Instead of a lot of computers doing a lot of jobs, one central, or main computer, will control all of the smaller jobs.

Due to the recession, companies are fighting for every little bit of business they can grab. Therefore, in today's rat race every little change might make a big difference. Companies believe that using one computer will save them money because one large computer can do more than one task at a time. Actually, it is considered the human version of multitasking. Furthermore, by moving toward virtualization, businesses can save energy. Businesses can reduce the number of computers, thus reducing the amount of energy that they use as a business, and saving additional time. With fewer machines there is less maintenance and time spent on maintenance can be spent elsewhere. With competition at an all-time high, small changes can make a big difference and virtualization meets this challenge that now faces the modern day business model. Only time will tell if the small change will have a big effect.

21. **How does the author feel about virtualization?**
(Rigorous)

   A. The author thinks that it is a great idea

   B. The author feels that it is the only way to handle the recession

   C. The author isn't convinced that the small change will have a big effect

   D. The author believes it should have been introduced a long time ago

22. **How does the author feel about today's business environment?**
(Rigorous)

   A. The author believes that it is difficult to succeed in today's business environment

   B. The author thinks that businesses have gotten too big

   C. The author feels that only people are capable of multitasking

   D. The author thinks that businesses rely too heavily on machines to do a human's work

23. **From this passage, one can infer that**
(*Rigorous*)

A. The economy is doing well and companies are spending their money wisely

B. The economy used to be doing better and consumers, as well as companies, have had to make adjustments

C. The stock market is what drives consumer confidence and company sales

D. Many companies do whatever other companies are doing

24. **From this passage, one can infer that**
(*Rigorous*)

A. Before the economy was doing poorly, companies focused their spending in other areas

B. Company workers are finding other jobs because of the bad economy

C. Employees will lose their jobs due to the recession

D. Companies are trying virtualization instead of resorting to employee lay offs to save money

Directions: Read the following passage and answer questions 25–31.

Megan was about to plant the last plant in the sunniest spot in the yard. She worked with the soft, pliable soil to steady the plant around the roots. She filled in the empty area around the roots with more dirt. Recently, Megan had decided that she was going to plant a butterfly garden in her yard. She had worked very hard over the past week to clear the area so she would be able to plant this week while her grandparents were visiting. She and her grandmother had just returned from the nursery where they bought some Petunias, Peonies, and Hollyhocks. Consequently, these plants would attract all sorts of butterflies.

25. **What is the main idea of the passage?**
(*Average*)

A. How to create a butterfly garden

B. Megan was in the final stages of creating her butterfly garden

C. Petunias, Peonies, and Hollyhocks need to be planted in a sunny spot

D. A butterfly garden is the name for a garden that contains Peonies

26. **Why did the author write this article?**
(Average)

   A. To convince the reader to plant a butterfly garden

   B. To teach the reader how to plant a butterfly garden

   C. To encourage the reader to spend time with their family

   D. To amuse the reader with a story about planting a garden

27. **How is the passage above organized?**
(Average)

   A. Sequence of events

   B. Cause and effect

   C. Statement support

   D. Compare and contrast

28. **What cause and effect relationship exists in this paragraph?**
(Rigorous)

   A. Because it is sunny, the butterflies will visit Megan's garden

   B. Because Megan worked so hard this week, her grandparents came to visit

   C. Because Megan planted certain plants, butterflies will like her garden

   D. Because it was sunny, Megan was planting her last plant

29. **By using the word *consequently* in the final sentence of the first paragraph, what is the author implying?**
(Rigorous)

   A. That Megan did not want butterflies to visit her garden

   B. Megan's grandmother did not want butterflies to visit the garden

   C. There would be consequences if the butterflies came to the garden

   D. The plants were purchased so that butterflies would visit the garden

30. **What transition word could the author have used to connect these two sentences?**
(Average)

She worked with the soft, <u>pliable</u> soil to steady the plant around the roots. She filled in the empty area around the roots with more dirt.

A. Third,

B. Hence,

C. Next,

D. Prior to that,

31. **What does the word *pliable* mean in the second sentence?**
(Average)

A. Wet

B. Organic

C. Bendable

D. Sandy

Directions: Read the following passage and answer questions 32–34.

The Fog and *The Hitchhiker* are both suspenseful. Both plays also contain ghost characters. Ghosts frighten me. *The Fog* has three ghost characters named Eben, Zeke, and a wounded man. The reader does not realize that these men are ghosts however, until the end of the play. In *The Hitchhiker*, there is one ghost character known as "The Gray Man" who stalks the main character, Ronald Adams, until the end of the play. It is not revealed however, who the hitchhiker is until the end. The reader needs to make their own decision about his significance. The Gray Man is a little creepy.

The Fog takes place in Gettysburg, Pennsylvania during a war. *The Hitchhiker* on the other hand, is a more modern play and takes place during the 1930s and 1940s as a traveler drives to many cities across the country.

32. **How is the above passage organized?**
(Average)

A. Compare and contrast

B. Cause and effect

C. Sequence of events

D. Statement support

33. **Which sentence in the passage above is irrelevant?**
(Average)

   A. *The Fog* and *The Hitchhiker* are both suspenseful.

   B. Both plays also contain ghost characters.

   C. Ghosts frighten me.

   D. *The Fog* has three ghost characters named Eben, Zeke, and a wounded man.

34. **Which sentence in the passage above is irrelevant?**
(Rigorous)

   A. The reader does not realize that these men are ghosts.

   B. In *The Hitchhiker* there is one ghost character known as "The Gray Man."

   C. It is not revealed who the hitchhiker is until the end of the play.

   D. The Gray Man is a little creepy.

Directions: Read the following passage and answer questions 35–36.

Smells were coming from the kitchen that repelled Kim further and further away. But he couldn't get far away enough to escape the odor. His sister Lee was experimenting with a new recipe. Lee often cooked new exotic and foreign dishes. Sometimes this was great for Kim because he was always the first one to try one of Lee's newest creations. He remembered the time that she made zesty fruit salsa with cinnamon pita chips. Maybe he could request that she make that again instead of what she was cooking now.

35. **What conclusion can be drawn from the above passage?**
(Rigorous)

   A. Kim is a good cook

   B. Lee enjoys cooking

   C. Kim doesn't enjoy Lee's cooking

   D. Lee only makes desserts

36. **What can be inferred about Kim and Lee's relationship from the passage above?**
(Rigorous)

    A. Overall, Kim and Lee get along

    B. Kim and Lee do not get along well

    C. Kim only tells Lee about dishes he doesn't like

    D. Kim and Lee only share an interest in cooking

Directions: Read the following passage and answer questions 37–40.

Have you ever heard the expression, "Busy as a bee"? Well, nothing could be more true. Bees are very busy insects, and they are very interesting. Bees live in colonies where each member has a specific job. In honeybee colonies, there are queens, drones, and workers. The queen is the largest bee and lays all the eggs. The drones do not have stingers, and their job is to mate with the queen. Most of the bees in the colony are workers. They care for the queen, remove trash, build the nest, guard the entrance, and collect nectar, pollen, and water. Sounds like most worker bees are males. The bees that go out to collect are called foragers.

37. **What is the main idea of the passage?**
(Average)

    A. Bees live in colonies

    B. There are three different types of bees

    C. Each type of bee has a specific job that is important to the colonies' survival

    D Foragers are also known as collectors and they have an important job

38. **What does the word _forage_ mean?**
    (Easy)

    A. Work hard

    B. To be busy

    C. To care for

    D. Go and collect

39. **Which is an opinion contained in this passage?**
    (Average)

    A. Bees are very interesting

    B. Bees live in colonies

    C. Each colony has a queen

    D. The queen is the largest bee

40. **From this article you can see that the author thinks**
    (Rigorous)

    A. Bees lay large eggs.

    B. Drones have the best job.

    C. Men work very hard.

    D. Foragers have the most important job.

BASIC SKILLS

WRITING

Directions: The passage below contains many errors. Read the passage. Then, answer each test item by choosing the option that corrects an error in the underlined portion(s). No more than one underlined error will appear in each item. If no error exists, choose "No change is necessary."

If you give me ten dollars, I'll give you fifty in return. Does this sound too good to be true? Well, anything that sounds too good to be true probably is. That stands true for herbal supplements. Herbal supplements are main targeted toward improving one type of ailment. There is no cure-all herbal supplement so don't believe what he tells you. Herbal supplement can fix more than one thing.

   Herbal supplements is great and have a lot of positive things to offer its takers and have become very popular with consumers. Many doctors are even suggesting that they try natural herbal remedies before prescribing an over-the-counter medication. Herbal supplements have given consumers a new power to self-diagnose and consumers can head to the health food store and pick up an herbal supplement rather than heading to the doctor. Herbal supplements take a little long than prescribed medication to clear up any illnesses, but they are a more natural way to go, and some consumers prefer that form of medication.

1. Herbal supplements are <u>main</u> targeted <u>toward improving</u> one type of ailment.
   (Average)

   A. mainly

   B. towards

   C. improve

   D. No change is necessary

2. There is <u>no</u> cure-all herbal <u>supplement</u> so don't believe what <u>he</u> tells you.
   (Easy)

   A. nothing

   B. supplemental

   C. you hear

   D. No change is necessary

3. Many doctors <u>are</u> even suggesting that <u>they</u> try natural herbal remedies before <u>prescribing</u> an over-the-counter medication.
   (Rigorous)

   A. is

   B. their patients

   C. prescribing,

   D. No change is necessary

4. **Herbal supplements <u>is</u> great and have <u>a lot</u> of positive things to offer <u>its</u> takers and have become very popular with consumers.**
(Easy)

A. are

B. alot

C. it's

D. No change is necessary

5. **Herbal supplements take a little <u>long</u> <u>than</u> <u>prescribed</u> medications to clear up any illnesses, but they are a more natural way to go, and some consumers prefer that form of medication.**
(Average)

A. longer

B. then

C. perscribed

D. No changes necessary

6. **Herbal <u>supplements</u> take a little long than prescribed <u>medication</u> to clear up any illnesses, but they are a <u>more natural</u> way to go, and some consumers prefer that form of medication.**
(Rigorous)

A. supplement

B. medications

C. more naturally

D. No change necessary

7. **Herbal <u>supplement</u> can fix more <u>than</u> one <u>thing</u>.**
(Average)

A. supplements

B. then

C. things

D. No change is necessary

Directions: The passage below contains many errors. Read the passage. Then, answer each test item by choosing the option that corrects an error in the underlined portion(s). No more than one underlined error will appear in each item. If no error exists, choose "No change is necessary."

Bingo has many purposes in the United States. It is used as a learning and entertainment tool for children. Bingo is used as an entertainment tool for parties and picnics to entertain a large number of people easily and quickly. Bingo is also a common game played among elderly and church groups because of its simplistic way of entertaining.

   A typical bingo card has the word "bingo" printed across the top with columns of numbers inside boxes underneath. There is a "free" space located directly in the middle. There is usually one person who calls the numbers. For example, a ball or chip may be labeled "B12." Players then look under the "B" column for the number 12 and if it appears on their card, they place a marker on top of it. If there isn't a 12 under the letter "B" on a player's card, then they simply wait for the next number to be called.

8. <u>Players</u> then look under the "B" column for the number 12 and if it appears on <u>his</u> card, <u>they</u> place a marker on top of it.
    (Rigorous)

    A. He

    B. their

    C. him

    D. No change is necessary

9. **Bingo is used as a learning and entertainment tool for children.**
    (Rigorous)

    A. Bingo is used as a learning tool and entertainment for children.

    B. Bingo is used for learning and entertainment for children.

    C. Bingo is used to both teach and entertain children.

    D. No change is necessary

10. **Players then look under the "B" column for the number 12 and if it appears on their card, they place a marker on top of it.**
(Rigorous)

A. Players then look under the, "B" column for the number 12, and if it appears on their card they place a marker on top of it.

B. Players then look under the "B" column for the number, 12, and if it appears on their card they place a marker on top of it.

C. Players then look under the "B" column for the number 12 and if it appears on their card they place a marker on top of it.

D. No change necessary

Directions: The passage below contains many errors. Read the passage. Then, answer each test item by choosing the option that corrects an error in the underlined portion(s). No more than one underlined error will appear in each item. If no error exists, choose "No change is necessary."

A family of four, consisting of two children and two adults, were trying to decide where they should go to have lunch at. Each of them wanted something different, so deciding between four places was not an easy task. The youngest child wanted fast food of course simply because they wanted to get the toy prize of the week. The eldest child was watching her weight and wanted to skip lunch altogether. The Mother was in the mood for a nice deli sandwich, one with many layers of ham and cheese. The father wanted a nice juicy burger—but not the kind from a fast food establishment. After much minutes of deliberating, the family decided to simply return home for leftover chicken from the night before.

11. **The youngest child wanted fast food of course simply because they wanted to get the toy prize of the week.**
(Average)

A. young

B. food, of course,

C. want

D. No change is necessary

12. The youngest <u>child</u> wanted fast food of course <u>simply</u> because <u>they</u> wanted to get the toy prize of the week.
(Average)

A. children

B. simple

C. she

D. No change is necessary

13. A family of <u>four, consisting</u> of two children and two adults, were trying to <u>decide</u> where they should go to have <u>lunch at.</u>
(Rigorous)

A. four consisting

B. deciding

C. lunch.

D. No change is necessary

14. <u>Each</u> of them wanted something different, so <u>deciding</u> <u>between</u> four places was not an easy task.
(Rigorous)

A. One

B. decided

C. among

D. No change is necessary

15. After <u>much</u> minutes of deliberating, the family <u>decided</u> to <u>simply</u> return home for leftover chicken from the night before.
(Average)

A. many

B. decides

C. simple

D. No change is necessary

16. <u>The Mother</u> was in the mood for a nice deli sandwich, one with <u>many</u> <u>layers</u> of ham and cheese.
(Easy)

A. The mother

B. much

C. layer

D. No change is necessary

Directions: The passage below contains many errors. Read the passage. Then, answer each test item by choosing the option that corrects an error in the underlined portion(s). No more than one underlined error will appear in each item. If no error exists, choose "No change is necessary."

California is known for many things. But do you know what dates back to 1874 when the gold minors invaded California? It's the tough as old boots, Levi's denim jeans. These jeans were originally made for the minors whom needed pants to withstand the rough terrain they often encountered. Levi Straus used heavy canvas fabric and brass ribbets in the seams to withstand the test of time. Not only are these jeans more tougher than any other denim jeans on the market for they are also very fashionable.

17. **Not only are these jeans <u>more tougher</u> than any other denim jeans on the <u>market for</u> they are also very fashionable.**
(Average)

    A. tougher

    B. then

    C. market, for

    D. No change is necessary

18. **<u>California</u> is known for <u>many things</u>.**
(Easy)

    A. California, is known...

    B. much

    C. things!

    D. No change is necessary

19. **These jeans were <u>originally</u> made for the <u>minors whom</u> needed pants to withstand <u>the rough terrain</u> they often encountered.**
(Rigorous)

    A. original

    B. miners who

    C. the rough terrain,

    D. No change is necessary.

20. These jeans were originally made for the miners who needed pants to withstand the rough terrain they often encountered.

How should this sentence be rewritten?
(Rigorous)

A. These jeans were originally made for the miners that needed pants to withstand the rough terrain. They often encountered.

B. The miners needed jeans that could withstand the rough terrain they often encountered.

C. These jeans were originally made for the rough terrain the miners needed.

D. These jeans were originally made to withstand the rough terrain that the miners often encountered.

21. Not only are these jeans tougher than any other denim jeans on the market for they are also very fashionable.
(Rigorous)

How should this sentence be rewritten?

A. Not only are these jeans tougher than any other denim jeans on the market, for they are also very fashionable.

B. Not only are these jeans tougher than any other denim jeans on the market but they are also more fashionable.

C. Not only are these jeans tougher than any other denim jeans on the market, but they are also very fashionable.

D. Not only, are these jeans tougher than any other denim jeans on the market, but, they are also very fashionable.

22. What does the idiom "tough as old boots" mean in the sentence, "It's the tough as old boots, Levi's denim jeans."
(Average)

A. Very rugged

B. Made of leather

C. As old as boots

D. Worn out and old

23. Levi Straus used heavy canvas fabric and brass ribbets in the seams to withstand the test of time.
(Easy)

Which word is used incorrectly in the sentence?

A. heavy

B. ribbets

C. seams

D. time

Directions: Read the following passage and answer questions 24–32.

I can't hardly believe that Kings dominion is opening again for the season this week. This season should be much more excitable because of the introduction of the new roller coaster—the Intimidator 305. Not only is it the 15th roller coaster that the park has ejected, but it is also the tallest and most fast coaster on the East Coast. The attendees of the park are looking forward to riding the newer roller coaster, that was concluded on January 9, 2010.

24. Not only is it the 15th roller coaster that the park has erected, but it is also the **tallest** and **most fast** coaster on the **East Coast.**
(Easy)

A. taller

B. fastest

C. East coast

D. No change is necessary

25. The <u>attendees</u> of the park <u>are</u> looking forward to riding the <u>newer</u> roller coaster, that was concluded on January 9, 2010.
(Average)

A. attendance

B. were

C. newest

D. No change is necessary

26. The season <u>should be</u> <u>much more</u> <u>excitable</u> because of the introduction of the new roller coaster.
(Average)

A. shouldn't be

B. more

C. exciting

D. No change is necessary

27. The attendees of the park are <u>looking</u> forward to riding the newest roller coaster that was <u>concluded</u> on <u>January 9, 2010.</u>
(Average)

A. looked

B. completed

C. January 9 2010

D. No change is necessary

28. I <u>can't hardly</u> believe that <u>Kings</u> dominion is opening again for the season this <u>week</u>.
(Easy)

A. can

B. King's

C. weekly

D. No change is necessary

29. <u>Not only</u> is it the 15th roller coaster that the park has <u>ejected</u>, but it is also the <u>tallest</u> and most fast coaster on the East Coast.
(Rigorous)

A. Not only,

B. erected

C. taller

D. No change is necessary

30. This season should be much more excitable because of the introduction of the <u>new roller coaster—the Intimidator 305.</u>
(Rigorous)

A. the new roller coaster, the Intimidator 305.

B. the new roller coaster—the Intimidator 305?

C. the new, roller coaster, the Intimidator 305.

D. No change is necessary

31. The attendees of the park are looking forward to riding the newest <u>roller coaster, that</u> was concluded on January 9, 2010. *(Rigorous)*

A. roller, coaster that

B. roller coaster that,

C. roller coaster that

D. No change is necessary

32. I can hardly believe that <u>Kings dominion</u> is opening again for the season this week. *(Average)*

A. King's dominion

B. Kings Dominion

C. kings dominion

D. No change is necessary

Directions: Read the following passage and answer questions 33–38.

It is a requirement that all parents volunteer two hours during the course of the season. Or an alternative was to pay $8 so you can have some high school students work a shift for you. Lots of parents liked this idea and will take advantage of the opportunity. Shifts run an hour long, and it is well worth it to pay the money so you don't miss your sons game.

33. It is a requirement that all parents volunteer two hours during the course of the season. *(Average)*

How should the above sentence be rewritten?

A. It is a requirement of all parents volunteering two hours during the course of the season.

B. It is required of all parents to volunteer for two hours during the course of the season.

C. They require all parents volunteer during the season.

D. Requiring all parents to volunteer for two hours over the course of the season.

34. An alternative <u>was</u> to pay $8 so you can have some <u>high school</u> students work a shift for you. *(Average)*

A. is

B. HighSchool

C. High school

D. No change is necessary

35. **Many parents liked this idea and will take advantage of the opportunity.**

    How should the sentence be rewritten?
    (Rigorous)

    A. Many parent's liked this idea and took advantage of the opportunity.

    B. Many parents like this idea and take advantage of the opportunity.

    C. Many parents like this idea and took advantage of the opportunity.

    D. Many parents did like this idea and take advantage of the opportunity.

36. **<u>Shifts</u> run an hour long, and it is well worth it <u>to</u> pay the money so you don't miss your <u>sons</u> games.**
    (Average)

    A. Shift's

    B. too

    C. son's

    D. No change is necessary

37. **It is a requirement that all <u>parents</u> volunteer two <u>hours</u> during the course of the season.**
    (Easy)

    A. parent's

    B. parents'

    C. hour's

    D. No change is necessary

38. **<u>Or an</u> alternative was to pay $8 so you can have some <u>high school</u> <u>students</u> work a shift for you.**
    (Rigorous)

    A. An

    B. high-school

    C. student's

    D. No change is necessary

Writing Essay

Although the marvels of technology surround us every day, there are moments when we all would give anything to be freed from that technology.

Discuss the extent to which you agree or disagree with this opinion. Support your views with specific reasons and examples from your own experience, observations, or reading.

MATH

1. **Which of the following is correct?**
   (Easy)

   A. 2365 > 2340

   B. 0.75 > 1.25

   C. 3/4 < 1/16

   D. -5 < -6

2. **Simplify:**

   $$\frac{5^{-2} \times 5^3}{5^5 \times 5^{-7}}$$

   (Average)

   A. 5^5

   B. 125

   C. $\dfrac{1}{125}$

   D. 25

3. **Choose the set in which the members are not equivalent.**
   (Average)

   A. 1/2, 0.5, 50%

   B. 10/5, 2.0, 200%

   C. 3/8, 0.385, 38.5%

   D. 7/10, 0.7, 70%

4. **The digit 8 in the number 975.086 is in the**
   (Easy)

   A. tenths place

   B. ones place

   C. hundredths place

   D. hundreds place

5. **The relations given below demonstrate the following addition and multiplication property of real numbers:**
   a + b = b + a
   ab = ba
   (Easy)

   A. Commutative

   B. Associative

   C. Identity

   D. Inverse

BASIC SKILLS

6. Simplify:

$$\frac{27 - 2.3^2}{8 \div 2^2 - (-2)^2}$$

(Rigorous)

A. 9/2

B. 9/8

C. -4.5

D. 0.75

7. At a publishing company, Mona can proofread 300 pages in 5 hours while Lisa can proofread 360 pages in 4 hours. If they share the task of proofreading a 375 page document, how long will it take them to complete the job?
(Rigorous)

A. 2.5 hours

B. 5 hours

C. 3 hours

D. 3.5 hours

8. A student had 60 days to appeal the results of an exam. If the results were received on March 23, what was the last day that the student could appeal?
(Average)

A. May 21

B. May 22

C. May 23

D. May 24

9. A coat is on sale for $135. If the discount offered is 25%, what was the original price of the coat?
(Rigorous)

A. $160

B. $180

C. $110

D. $150

10. If three cups of concentrate are needed to make 2 gallons of fruit punch, how many cups are needed to make 5 gallons?
(Average)

A. 6 cups

B. 7 cups

C. 7.5 cups

D. 10 cups

11. A sofa sells for $520. If the retailer makes a 30% profit, what was the wholesale price?
(*Average*)

A. $400

B. $676

C. $490

D. $364

12. What is the negation of a statement of the form "p and q"?
(*Average*)

A. Not and not q

B. Not p and q

C. Not p or not q

D. p or not q

13. The contrapositive of the statement "If I am hungry I eat" is:
(*Average*)

A. If I eat then I am hungry

B. If I am not hungry I do not eat

C. If I do not eat I am not hungry

D. None of the above

14. Solve for x:

$$3(5 + 3x) - 8 = 88$$

(*Average*)

A. 30

B. 9

C. 4.5

D. 27

15. Solve for x:

$$|2x + 3| > 4$$

(*Rigorous*)

A. $-\frac{7}{2} > x > \frac{1}{2}$

B. $-\frac{1}{2} > x > \frac{7}{2}$

C. $x < \frac{7}{2}$ or $x < -\frac{1}{2}$

D. $X < -\frac{7}{2}$ or $x > \frac{1}{2}$

BASIC SKILLS

16. You are helping students list the steps needed to solve the word problem:
"Mr. Jones is 5 times as old as his son. Two years later he will be 4 times as old as his son. How old is Mr. Jones?"

One of the students makes the following list:

1. Assume Mr. Jones' son is x years old. Express Mr. Jones' age in terms of x.
2. Write how old they will be two years later in terms of x.
3. Solve the equation for x.
4. Multiply the answer by 5 to get Mr. Jones' age.

What step is missing between steps 2 and 3?
(Rigorous)

A. Write an equation setting Mr. Jones age equal to 5 times his son's age

B. Write an equation setting Mr. Jones age two years later equal to 5 times his son's age two years later

C. Write an equation setting Mr. Jones age equal to 4 times his son's age

D. Write an equation setting Mr. Jones age two years later equal to 4 times his son's age two years later

17. The following equation is the best choice for teaching use of the distributive law in solving equations:
(Rigorous)

A. $3(x + 5) = 4x$

B. $x(3 + 5) = 4$

C. $4(x + 2x) = 2$

D. None of the above

18. What is the next term in the sequence

0.005, 0.03, 0.18, 1.08,…

(Rigorous)

A. 1.96

B. 2.16

C. 3.32

D. 6.48

19. {1,4,7,10, . . .}

What is the 40th term in this sequence?
(Average)

A. 43

B. 121

C. 118

D. 120

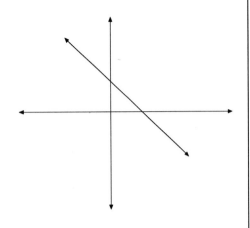

20. Which equation is represented by the above graph?
(Average)

A. x − y = 3

B. x − y = −3

C. x + y = 3

D. x + y = −3

21. Graph the solution:

|x| + 7 < 13

(Average)

A)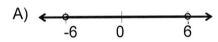

B)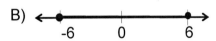

C)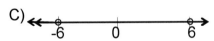

D)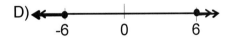

22. Which of the following shapes is not a parallelogram?
(Easy)

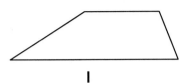

I

II

III

A. I & III

B. II & III

C. I

D. I, II & III

23. An isosceles triangle has:
(Easy)

A. Three equal sides

B. Two equal sides

C. No equal sides

D. Two equal sides in some cases, no equal sides in others

BASIC SKILLS

24. Given similar polygons with corresponding sides of lengths 9 and 15, find the perimeter of the smaller polygon if the perimeter of the larger polygon is 150 units.
(Rigorous)

A. 54

B. 135

C. 90

D. 126

25. Ginny and Nick head back to their respective colleges after being home for the weekend. They leave their house at the same time and drive for 4 hours. Ginny drives due south at the average rate of 60 miles per hour, and Nick drives due east at the average rate of 60 miles per hour. What is the straight-line distance between them, in miles, at the end of the 4 hours?
(Rigorous)

A. $120\sqrt{2}$

B. 240

C. $240\sqrt{2}$

D. 288

26. Given segment AC with B as its midpoint find the coordinates of C if A = (5,7) and B = (3, 6.5).
(Rigorous)

A. (4, 6.5)

B. (1, 6)

C. (2, 0.5)

D. (16, 1)

27. The following set of points on a coordinate plane define an isosceles right triangle
(Rigorous)

A. (4,0), (0,4), (4,4)

B. (4,0), (0,6), (4,4)

C. (0,0), (0,4), (5,2)

D. (0,0), (5.0), (5,2)

28. The speed of light in space is about 3×10^8 meters per second. Express this in Kilometers per hour.
(Average)

A. 1.08×10^9 Km / hr

B. 3.0×10^{11} Km / hr

C. 1.08×10^{12} Km / hr

D. 1.08×10^{15} Km / hr

BASIC SKILLS

29. Given a 30 meter x 60 meter garden with a circular fountain with a 5 meter radius, calculate the area of the portion of the garden not occupied by the fountain.
(Rigorous)

    A. 1721 m²

    B. 1879 m²

    C. 2585 m²

    D. 1015 m²

30. What is the length of a fourth of the circumference of a circle with a diameter of 24 cm?
(Rigorous)

    A. 18.85

    B. 75.4

    C. 32.45

    D. 20.75

31. What percentage of students got a C grade?
(Average)

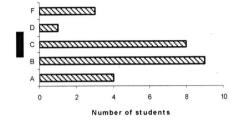

    A. 35

    B. 8

    C. 32

    D. 40

BASIC SKILLS

32. Which statement is true about George's budget?
(Easy)

A. George spends the greatest portion of his income on food

B. George spends twice as much on utilities as he does on his mortgage

C. George spends twice as much on utilities as he does on food

D. George spends the same amount on food and utilities as he does on mortgage

33. You are creating a pie chart to show the expenses for a business. If employee pay is 40% of the total expenditure, what central angle will you use to show that segment of the pie chart?
(Average)

A. 72°

B. 80°

C. 40°

D. 144°

34. Which of the following is the most accurate inference that can be made from the graph shown below?
(Average)

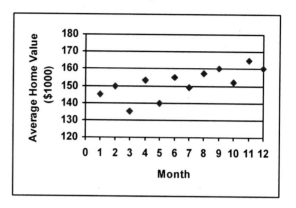

A. The average home value shows a decreasing trend over the 12-month period

B. The average home value shows an increasing trend over the 12-month period

C. The average home value stays about the same over the 12-month period

D. The data fluctuates too much to make any comment about the trend

35. Melissa scores 60, 68, and 75 in the first three of five tests. What should her average score be for the last two tests so that her mean test score for the 5 tests is 70?
(Rigorous)

A. 70

B. 73.5

C. 75.5

D. 85

36. Find the median of the following set of data:

14 3 7 6 11 20

(Easy)

A. 9

B. 8.5

C. 7

D. 11

37. Corporate salaries are listed for several employees. Which would be the best measure of central tendency?

| $24,000 | $24,000 | $26,000 |
| $28,000 | $30,000 | $120,000 |

(Average)

A. mean

B. median

C. mode

D. no difference

38. A jar contains 3 red marbles, 5 white marbles, 1 green marble and 15 blue marbles. If one marble is picked at random from the jar, what is the probability that it will be red?
(Easy)

A. $\dfrac{1}{3}$

B. $\dfrac{1}{8}$

C. $\dfrac{3}{8}$

D. $\dfrac{1}{24}$

39. Given a drawer with 5 black socks, 3 blue socks, and 2 red socks, what is the probability that you will draw two black socks in two draws in a dark room?
(Rigorous)

A. 2/9

B. 1/4

C. 17/18

D. 1/18

40. A sack of candy has 3 peppermints, 2 butterscotch drops and 3 cinnamon drops. One candy is drawn and replaced, then another candy is drawn; what is the probability that both will be butterscotch?
(Rigorous)

A. 1/2

B. 1/28

C. 1/4

D. 1/16

BASIC SKILLS

Answer Key: Reading

1.	D	21.	C
2.	D	22.	A
3.	A	23.	B
4.	C	24.	A
5.	D	25.	B
6.	A	26.	D
7.	D	27.	A
8.	D	28.	C
9.	B	29.	D
10.	A	30.	C
11.	D	31.	C
12.	B	32.	A
13.	B	33.	C
14.	B	34.	D
15.	B	35.	B
16.	A	36.	A
17.	A	37.	C
18.	B	38.	D
19.	D	39.	A
20.	A	40.	C

Rigor Table: Reading

	Easy 20%	Average 40%	Rigorous 40%
Questions	8, 9, 10, 15, 16, 17, 18, 38	1, 2, 4, 7, 11, 13, 20, 25, 26, 27, 30, 31, 32, 33, 37, 39	3, 5, 6, 12, 14, 19, 21, 22, 23, 24, 28, 29, 34, 35, 36, 40

READING

Directions: Read the following passage and answer question 1–8.

The Eiffel Tower in Paris, France, is probably the country's most recognizable symbol. Not only is the tower an obvious symbol, but it is also an incredible work of art that was designed by Gustave Eiffel. The tower, which was opened March 31, 1889, was originally built for the Universal Exhibition and was only meant to stand for twenty years then be destroyed. Luckily, the tower still stands to this day in the original post it was constructed.

Between 1889 when the tower opened and December 31, 2008, 243,376,000 people have visited the 324-meter, iron tower. In order to ride to the second floor of the tower, a visitor must pay 8 francs to ride the elevator. To ride all the way to the top floor, a visitor must pay 13 francs. For only 4.50 francs, a visitor can take the stairs. Unfortunately, guests must climb 115 meters to reach the second floor, and stairs are not available for visitors who wish to go to the top of the tower. In other words, visitors who wish to go all the way to the top of the tower must take the elevator.

1. **What is the main idea of the passage?**
   (Average)

   A.   The Eiffel Tower opened on March 31, 1889

   B.   Many people have visited the Eiffel Tower since it opened

   C.   Visitors can take the elevator or the stairs to reach the top of the tower

   D.   The Eiffel Tower is a well-known symbol around the world

Answer: D. The Eiffel Tower is a well-known symbol around the world
Choices A, B, and C are all details that are very specific and support the main idea that the Eiffel Tower is a well-known symbol around the world.

2. **Why did the author write this article?**
   (Average)

   A.   To entertain

   B.   To persuade

   C.   To describe

   D.   To inform

Answer: D. To inform
The author wrote this article to teach its readers about the Eiffel Tower—in other words to inform them.

3. **What is the best summary of the second paragraph?**
   (Rigorous)

   A.   Visitors can ride an elevator or take the stairs to reach certain heights of the Eiffel Tower

   B.   The Eiffel Tower is very tall and stands 324 meters high

   C.   The elevator at the Eiffel Tower only reaches 115 meters

   D.   Visitors must pay in order to climb to the top of the Eiffel Tower

Answer: A. Visitors can ride an elevator or take the stairs to reach certain heights of the Eiffel Tower
Choices B, C, and D are all details that support the main idea of the second paragraph.

4. **How is the passage above organized?**
   (Average)

   A.   Cause and effect

   B.   Compare and contrast

   C.   Statement support

   D.   Sequence of events

Answer: C. Statement support
The main idea of each paragraph is stated and then supporting sentences follow. Therefore, this is a "statement support" organization example.

5. **What comparison is made in the first paragraph?**
   (Rigorous)

   A.   The Eiffel Tower is in Paris, France but is enjoyed by the world

   B.   The Eiffel Tower opened in 1889 and is still in the same spot today

   C.   The Eiffel Tower is recognizable and it serves as a country's symbol

   D.   The Eiffel Tower is a great symbol of France and a work of art

Answer: D. The Eiffel Tower is a great symbol of France and a work of art
The author is saying that the Eiffel Tower is both France's most recognized symbol and a work of art that was created in 1889 and is still in its original spot for all to enjoy.

6. **By using the word *luckily* in the final sentence of the first paragraph, what is the author implying?**
    (Rigorous)

    A. That tearing the tower down as originally intended would have been a bad decision

    B. It is a good thing for France that the tower remains in the same spot it was built

    C. If the tower had been torn down, Gustave, its designer would have been angry

    D. The Universal Exhibition can now take place in the exact same spot someday since the tower remains

Answer: A. That tearing the tower down as originally intended would have been a bad decision
By using the transition word *luckily* to begin the last sentence in the first paragraph, the author is implying that it was a good decision to leave the tower in its original spot and not destroy it as was originally planned so that future generations might enjoy its artistic beauty.

7. **What words does the author use in paragraph 2 to clarify information for the reader?**
    (Average)

    A. Between

    B. In order to

    C. Unfortunately

    D. In other words

Answer: D. In other words
The phrase *in other words* is a great transition that authors often use to clarify information stated in a previous sentence. Here, the author wants to draw the reader's attention to the fact that stairs do not run all the way to the top of the Eiffel Tower, and it is necessary for visitors to pay 13 francs to ride the elevator to the top.

BASIC SKILLS

8. **What would have been the best transition word for the author to use to connect these two sentences?**
(Easy)

In order to ride to the second floor of the tower, a visitor must pay 8 francs to ride the elevator. To ride all the way to the top floor, a visitor must pay 13 francs.

A.   Next,

B.   Beyond,

C.   For example,

D.   Consequently,

Answer: D. Consequently,
Choice A will not work because *next* is a transition word that shows time. *Beyond,* Choice B, shows a place. Choice C will not work because the author is not giving an example. However, Choice D, *consequently* is the best fit because it helps get the idea across that if a visitor paid 8 francs to ride the elevator to the second floor, they would then have to pay a bit more to ride all the way to the top.

9. **What does the word *pang* mean in the sentence below?**
(Easy)

Standing outside of her homeroom, Lauren watched other children enter the room and overheard them sharing stories about their summer adventures. She couldn't help but feel a <u>pang</u> of loneliness as she thought of her best friend Morgan back in Colorado.

A.   Pain

B.   Hint

C.   Depression

D.   Song

Answer: B. Hint
The student feels a little bit lonely as she adjusts to a new school without her best friend from where she used to live.

10. **What does the word *convoluted* mean in the sentence below?**
(Easy)

Misty listened to Marty intently. But as Marty revealed more of her plan, Misty wasn't sure she wanted anything to do with it. Marty's plan was <u>convoluted</u> and twisted and, quite frankly, Misty was worried about her own safety.

    A.   Strange

    B.   Straight

    C.   Thorough

    D.   Polluted

Answer: A. Strange
The author gives clarification for the word *convoluted* by adding the word "twisted" to the sentence. Therefore, the reader knows that the plan is strange and twisted because *strange* is a synonym of twisted in this context.

11. **The book *The Giver* by Lois Lowry is a great book. The characters are interesting and they are unique. Everyone who reads *The Giver* will enjoy it and not be able to put it down.**

Is this a valid or invalid argument?
(Average)

    A.   Valid

    B.   Invalid

Answer: B. Invalid
The author does not support their opinions with any evidence or facts from the story.

12. I-95 is the best route to take from Virginia to Washington, DC. There are many rest stops along the way so it is easy to stop and get gas, food, and use the restrooms when necessary. There is also an HOV lane that allows those traveling with others to bypass single traveler cars.

Is this a valid or invalid argument?
(Average)

A.   Valid

B.   Invalid

Answer: A. Valid
The author supports their opinions with evidence and facts.

13. **Which sentence in the passage below is irrelevant?**
(Rigorous)

Cats was one of the longest running musicals. It opened October 7, 1982, at the Winter Garden Theater in New York City. New York City is also known as Manhattan. The music, which has become very popular and well-known, was written by Andrew Lloyd Webber. He grew up in London, England. Perhaps the best-known hit was "Memory," which became popular world wide, and was recorded in more than twelve languages. The actual story is based on the book *Old Possum's Book of Practical Cats* written by T.S. Eliot, which is a series of children's poems.

A.   *Cats* was one of the longest running musicals

B.   It opened October 7, 1982 at the Winter Garden Theater

C.   New York City is also known as Manhattan

D.   The music is popular and well-known and was written by Andrew Lloyd Webber

Answer: C. New York City is also known as Manhattan
The idea that New York City is also known as Manhattan does not support the main idea of the passage. Therefore, it is irrelevant.

BASIC SKILLS

14. **Which sentence in the passage above is irrelevant?**
   (Rigorous)

   A.   The music, which has become very popular and well-known, was written by Andrew Lloyd Webber

   B.   He grew up in London, England

   C.   Perhaps the best-known hit was "Memory" which became popular world wide

   D.   The actual story is based on the book *Old Possum's Book of Practical Cats.*

Answer: B. He grew up in London, England
The idea that Webber grew up in London, England, does not support the main idea of the passage. Therefore, it is irrelevant.

15. **Elementary school is better than middle school. Is this sentence a fact or an opinion?**
   (Easy)

   A.   Fact

   B.   Opinion

Answer: B. Opinion
It depends on one's personal experience whether elementary or middle school is better.

16. **Letter grades are given at Thomas Jefferson Middle School. Is this sentence a fact or an opinion?**
   (Easy)

   A.   Fact

   B.   Opinion

Answer: A. Fact
It can be proved whether Thomas Jefferson Middle School gives letter grades.

17. **The science fair will take place at 4:00 on Saturday, March 13. Is this sentence a fact or an opinion?**
(Easy)

    A.   Fact

    B.   Opinion

Answer: A. Fact
The time and place that something occurs is a fact because it can be proven.

18. **The science fair will be a lot of fun so everyone should attend. Is this sentence a fact or an opinion?**
(Easy)

    A.   Fact

    B.   Opinion

Answer: B. Opinion
It is up to individual attendees whether it was fun to attend the science fair. Therefore, it is an opinion.

19. *Thank you so much for the gift you sent for my birthday. It was nice of you to send me a gift and remember that my birthday was last week. Your generosity is appreciated. Thanks again.*
                                John

    What conclusion can be drawn from the above letter?
(Rigorous)

    A.   The author and the gift giver are related

    B.   The author is a child that received a gift

    C.   The gift was a toy and the author liked it

    D.   The author didn't really like the gift

Answer: D. The author didn't really like the gift
Choices A, B, and C might be true, but there isn't anything in the letter to support any of these ideas. Because nothing specific is addressed in the letter, it is acceptable to conclude that the author didn't really like the gift.

BASIC SKILLS

20. *Even after turning the lock correctly it still wouldn't open. My combination is 32-41-12; I hope this will help you get to the bottom of the problem. All of my school supplies are locked inside, and I must have them in order to be successful in my classes.*

What conclusion can be drawn from the paragraph above?
(Average)

A.   A teacher's belongings are locked inside of her car

B.   A student is having trouble with their locker

C.   A student's gym locker is jammed

D.   A traveler's locker is jammed

Answer: B. A student is having trouble with their locker
The student's class supplies are in their locker, which they can't open because of problems with the combination lock.

Directions: Read the following passage and answer questions 21–24.

It is not news to anyone who has been following the changes in the economy that people are spending less. This is a wise decision by all consumers and since people are reevaluating their spending, it is necessary for companies to reevaluate their plans for growth. Many companies that were spending money on security have had to shift their focus elsewhere. A number of companies have made the decision to focus on virtualization—when one computer completes the jobs of many. Instead of a lot of computers doing a lot of jobs, one central, or main computer, will control all of the smaller jobs.

   Due to the recession, companies are fighting for every little bit of business they can grab. Therefore, in today's rat race every little change might make a big difference. Companies believe that using one computer will save them money because one large computer can do more than one task at a time. Actually, it is considered the human version of multitasking. Furthermore, by moving toward virtualization, businesses can save energy. Businesses can reduce the number of computers, thus reducing the amount of energy that they use as a business, and saving additional time. With fewer machines there is less maintenance and time spent on maintenance can be spent elsewhere. With competition at an all-time high, small changes can make a big difference and virtualization meets this challenge that now faces the modern day business model. Only time will tell if the small change will have a big effect.

21. How does the author feel about virtualization?
(Rigorous)

    A.   The author thinks that it is a great idea

    B.   The author feels that it is the only way to handle the recession

    C.   The author isn't convinced that the small change will have a big effect

    D.   The author believes it should have been introduced a long time ago.

Answer: C. The author isn't convinced that the small change will have a big effect
The last sentence of the selection tells us that the author is not convinced that the small change will have a big effect on businesses.

22. How does the author feel about today's business environment?
(Rigorous)

    A.   The author believes that it is difficult to succeed in today's business environment

    B.   The author thinks that businesses have gotten too big

    C.   The author feels that only people are capable of multi-tasking

    D.   The author thinks that businesses rely too heavily on machines to do a human's work

Answer: A. The author believes that it is difficult to succeed in today's business environment
The first two sentences of the second paragraph use words like "fighting" and "rat race" to describe today's business environment. Therefore, you can tell that the author feels that it is difficult for businesses to succeed these days.

23. **From this passage, one can infer that**
    (Rigorous)

    A.   The economy is doing well and companies are spending their money wisely

    B.   The economy used to be doing better and consumers, as well as companies, have had to make adjustments

    C.   The stock market is what drives consumer confidence and company sales

    D.   Many companies do whatever other companies are doing

Answer: B. The economy used to be doing better and consumers, as well as companies, have had to make adjustments
This article is all about consumers and companies having to change the way they spend because of the status of the economy.

24. **From this passage, one can infer that**
    (Rigorous)

    A.   Before the economy was doing poorly, companies focused their spending in other areas

    B.   Company workers are finding other jobs because of the bad economy

    C.   Employees will lose their jobs due to the recession

    D.   Companies are trying virtualization instead of resorting to employee lay offs to save money

Answer: A. Before the economy was doing poorly, companies focused their spending in other areas
Although B, C, and D are feasible choices, there isn't anything in the article that gives any indication that any of these choices would take place. Therefore, choice A is the best choice.

Directions: Read the following passage and answer questions 25–31.

Megan was about to plant the last plant in the sunniest spot in the yard. She worked with the soft, <u>pliable</u> soil to steady the plant around the roots. She filled in the empty area around the roots with more dirt. Recently, Megan had decided that she was going to plant a butterfly garden in her yard. She had worked very hard over the past week to clear the area so she would be able to plant this week while her grandparents were visiting. She and her grandmother had just returned from the nursery where they bought some Petunias, Peonies, and Hollyhocks. Consequently, these plants would attract all sorts of butterflies.

25. **What is the main idea of the passage?**
    (Average)

    A.   How to create a butterfly garden

    B.   Megan was in the final stages of creating her butterfly garden

    C.   Petunias, Peonies, and Hollyhocks need to be planted in a sunny spot

    D.   A butterfly garden is the name for a garden that contains Peonies

Answer: B. Megan was in the final stages of creating her butterfly garden
The main idea of a fiction passage is also its summary. A good summary for this passage is Choice B, "Megan was in the final stages of creating her butterfly garden."

26. **Why did the author write this article?**
    (Average)

    A.   To convince the reader to plant a butterfly garden

    B.   To teach the reader how to plant a butterfly garden

    C.   To encourage the reader to spend time with their family

    D.   To amuse the reader with a story about planting a garden

Answer: D. To amuse the reader with a story about planting a garden
This was written to entertain. Amuse is a synonym for entertain. Therefore, it is the best choice.

27. **How is the passage above organized?**
    (Average)

    A. Sequence of events

    B. Cause and effect

    C. Statement support

    D. Compare and contrast

Answer: A. Sequence of events
This narrative tells events in order.

28. **What cause and effect relationship exists in this paragraph?**
    (Rigorous)

    A. Because it is sunny, the butterflies will visit Megan's garden

    B. Because Megan worked so hard this week, her grandparents came to visit

    C. Because Megan planted certain plants, butterflies will like her garden

    D. Because it was sunny, Megan was planting her last plant

Answer: C. Because Megan planted certain plants, butterflies will like her garden
Petunias, Peonies, and Hollyhocks are plants butterflies are attracted to.
Because Megan planted these, butterflies will be attracted to her garden.

29. **By using the word *consequently* in the final sentence of the first paragraph, what is the author implying?**
    (Rigorous)

    A.   That Megan did not want butterflies to visit her garden

    B.   Megan's grandmother did not want butterflies to visit the garden

    C.   There would be consequences if the butterflies came to the garden

    D.   The plants were purchased so that butterflies would visit the garden

Answer: D. The plants were purchased so that butterflies would visit the garden
Megan wants the butterflies to come to the garden and that is the reason that she purchased the types of plants that she did.

30. **What transition word could the author have used to connect these two sentences?**
    (Average)

    She worked with the soft, <u>pliable</u> soil to steady the plant around the roots. She filled in the empty area around the roots with more dirt.

    A.   Third,

    B.   Hence,

    C.   Next,

    D.   Prior to that,

Answer: C. Next,
"Next" shows time and works because Megan first settled the plant roots into the soil and then filled in the area around it. Choices A and C won't work because they are not the correct sequence word. The word *hence* means *because*.

31. **What does the word *pliable* mean in the second sentence?**
    (Average)

    A.   Wet

    B.   Organic

    C.   Bendable

    D.   Sandy

Answer: C. Bendable
Megan was able to mold the soil around the roots of the plants because it was bendable.

Directions: Read the following passage and answer questions 32–34.

The Fog and *The Hitchhiker* are both suspenseful. Both plays also contain ghost characters. Ghosts frighten me. *The Fog* has three ghost characters named Eben, Zeke, and a wounded man. The reader does not realize that these men are ghosts however, until the end of the play. In *The Hitchhiker*, there is one ghost character known as "The Gray Man" who stalks the main character, Ronald Adams, until the end of the play. It is not revealed however, who the hitchhiker is until the end. The reader needs to make their own decision about his significance. The Gray Man is a little creepy.

    The Fog takes place in Gettysburg, Pennsylvania during a war. *The Hitchhiker* on the other hand, is a more modern play and takes place during the 1930s and 1940s as a traveler drives to many cities across the country.

32. **How is the above passage organized?**
    (Average)

    A.   Compare and contrast

    B.   Cause and effect

    C.   Sequence of events

    D.   Statement support

Answer: A. Compare and contrast
This passage compares (gives similarities) and contrasts (shows differences) between two plays, *The Fog* and *The Hitchhiker*.

33. Which sentence in the passage above is irrelevant?
   (Average)

   A.   *The Fog* and *The Hitchhiker* are both suspenseful.

   B.   Both plays also contain ghost characters.

   C.   Ghosts frighten me.

   D.   *The Fog* has three ghost characters named Eben, Zeke, and a wounded man.

Answer: C. Ghosts frighten me.
The passage is talking about ghost characters that are in two plays. To interject personal feelings about ghosts is irrelevant.

34. Which sentence in the passage above is irrelevant?
   (Rigorous)

   A.   The reader does not realize that these men are ghosts.

   B.   In *The Hitchhiker*, there is one ghost character known as "The Gray Man."

   C.   It is not revealed who the hitchhiker is until the end of the play.

   D.   The Gray Man is a little creepy.

Answer: D. The Gray Man is a little creepy.
This is the author's personal opinion about the Gray Man and is irrelevant to the passage.

Directions: Read the following passage and answer questions 35–36.

Smells were coming from the kitchen that repelled Kim further and further away. But he couldn't get far away enough to escape the odor. His sister Lee was experimenting with a new recipe. Lee often cooked new exotic and foreign dishes. Sometimes this was great for Kim because he was always the first one to try one of Lee's newest creations. He remembered the time that she made zesty fruit salsa with cinnamon pita chips. Maybe he could request that she make that again instead of what she was cooking now.

35. **What conclusion can be drawn from the above passage?**
    (Rigorous)

    A.   Kim is a good cook

    B.   Lee enjoys cooking

    C.   Kim doesn't enjoy Lee's cooking

    D.   Lee only makes desserts

Answer- B. Lee enjoys cooking
There isn't anything in the passage to support Choices A and D. Choice C isn't always true—we know that Kim enjoyed Lee's fruit salsa and cinnamon pita chips. Therefore, Choice B is the best answer because the passage says that Lee likes to experiment in the kitchen.

36. **What can be inferred about Kim and Lee's relationship from the passage above?**
    (Rigorous)

    A.   Overall, Kim and Lee get along

    B.   Kim and Lee do not get along well

    C.   Kim only tells Lee about dishes he doesn't like

    D.   Kim and Lee only share an interest in cooking

Answer: A. Overall, Kim and Lee get along
It can be inferred from the passage that Kim and Lee have an overall good relationship. Lee enjoys cooking for Kim, and Kim enjoys trying Lee's experiments—most of the time.

Directions: Read the following passage and answer questions 37–40.

Have you ever heard the expression "Busy as a bee"? Well, nothing could be more true. Bees are very busy insects, and they are very interesting. Bees live in colonies where each member has a specific job. In honeybee colonies, there are queens, drones, and workers. The queen is the largest bee and lays all the eggs. The drones do not have stingers, and their job is to mate with the queen. Most of the bees in the colony are workers. They care for the queen, remove trash, build the nest, guard the entrance, and collect nectar, pollen, and water. Sounds like most worker bees are males. The bees that go out to collect are called foragers.

37. What is the main idea of the passage?
(Average)

    A.   Bees live in colonies

    B.   There are three different types of bees

    C.   Each type of bee has a specific job that is important to the colonies' survival

    D.   Foragers are also known a collectors and they have an important job

Answer: C. Each type of bee has a specific job that is important to the colonies' survival
Choices A, B, and D are all supporting details of the main idea, choice C.

38. What does the word *forage* mean?
(Easy)

    A.   Work hard

    B.   To be busy

    C.   To care for

    D.   Go and collect

Answer: D. Go and collect
The final sentence of the passage includes a context clue. It says, "the bees go out to collect and they are called foragers." This is because of the job they do.

39. **Which is an opinion contained in this passage?**
    (Average)

    A.   Bees are very interesting

    B.   Bees live in colonies

    C.   Each colony has a queen

    D.   The queen is the largest bee

Answer: A. Bees are very interesting
Choice A is the only choice that can be argued. Therefore, it is an opinion.

40. **From this article you can see that the author thinks**
    (Rigorous)

    A.   Bees lay large eggs

    B.   Drones have the best job

    C.   Men work very hard

    D.   Foragers have the most important job

Answer: C. Men work very hard
The author makes the statement "Sounds like most worker bees are males." By including this statement, the author is stating their opinion about how much work men do.

WRITING

Directions: The passage below contains many errors. Read the passage. Then, answer each test item by choosing the option that corrects an error in the underlined portion(s). No more than one underlined error will appear in each item. If no error exists, choose "No change is necessary."

If you give me ten dollars, I'll give you fifty in return. Does this sound too good to be true? Well, anything that sounds too good to be true probably is. That stands true for herbal supplements. Herbal supplements are main targeted toward improving one type of ailment. There is no cure-all herbal supplement so don't believe what he tells you. Herbal supplement can fix more than one thing.

Herbal supplements is great and have a lot of positive things to offer its takers and have become very popular with consumers. Many doctors are even suggesting that they try natural herbal remedies before prescribing an over-the-counter medication. Herbal supplements have given consumers a new power to self-diagnose and consumers can head to the health food store and pick up an herbal supplement rather than heading to the doctor. Herbal supplements take a little long than prescribed medication to clear up any illnesses, but they are a more natural way to go, and some consumers prefer that form of medication.

1. Herbal supplements are <u>main</u> targeted <u>toward improving</u> one type of ailment.
    (Average)

    A.   mainly

    B.   towards

    C.   improve

    D.   No change is necessary

Answer: A. mainly
Choice B doesn't work because the correct form of the word is indeed "toward." The gerund improving is necessary in the sentence. Therefore, Choice A, "mainly," is the correct adverb needed.

2. There is <u>no</u> cure-all herbal <u>supplement</u> so don't believe what <u>he</u> tells you.
(Easy)

   A.   nothing

   B.   supplemental

   C.   you hear

   D.   No change is necessary

Answer: C. you hear
As the sentence reads now, "he" is a pronoun that doesn't refer to anyone. Therefore, it shouldn't be used at all.

3. Many doctors <u>are</u> even suggesting that <u>they</u> try natural herbal remedies before <u>prescribing</u> an over-the-counter medication.
(Rigorous)

   A.   is

   B.   their patients

   C.   prescribing,

   D.   No change is necessary

Answer: B. their patients
The pronoun "they" is used incorrectly because it implies that the doctors should try natural herbal remedies. However, "they" is being used to take the place of their patients but has not been introduced prior to this point in the passage.

4. Herbal supplements <u>is</u> great and have <u>a lot</u> of positive things to offer <u>its</u> takers and have become very popular with consumers.
    (Easy)

    A.   are

    B.   alot

    C.   it's

    D.   No change is necessary

Answer: A. are
The linking verb must agree with the word supplements which is plural. Therefore, the correct verb must be "are" not "is."

5. Herbal supplements take a little <u>long</u> <u>than</u> <u>prescribed</u> medications to clear up any illnesses, but they are a more natural way to go, and some consumers prefer that form of medication.
    (Average)

    A.   longer

    B.   then

    C.   perscribed

    D.   No changes necessary

Answer A: longer
The sentence is comparing two things—herbal supplements to prescribed medications. The comparative form of the adjective "long" needs to be used and should be "longer."

6. Herbal <u>supplements</u> take a little long than prescribed <u>medication</u> to clear up any illnesses, but they are a <u>more natural</u> way to go, and some consumers prefer that form of medication.
   (Rigorous)

    A.   supplement

    B.   medications

    C.   more naturally

    D.   No change necessary

Answer: B. medications
Since the sentence begins talking about herbal supplements—plural—the comparison, prescribe medications, must be the same and be a plural too.

7. Herbal <u>supplement</u> can fix more <u>than</u> one <u>thing</u>.
   (Average)

    A.   supplements

    B.   then

    C.   things

    D.   No change is necessary

Answer: A. supplements
The article talks about herbal supplements and therefore must agree at all times throughout the article. Choice B is incorrect because then indicates that something happens next. "Than" is the correct word used in comparisons.

Directions: The passage below contains many errors. Read the passage. Then, answer each test item by choosing the option that corrects an error in the underlined portion(s). No more than one underlined error will appear in each item. If no error exists, choose "No change is necessary."

Bingo has many purposes in the United States. It is used as a learning and entertainment tool for children. Bingo is used as an entertainment tool for parties and picnics to entertain a large number of people easily and quickly. Bingo is also a common game played among elderly and church groups because of its simplistic way of entertaining.

A typical bingo card has the word "bingo" printed across the top with columns of numbers inside boxes underneath. There is a "free" space located directly in the middle. There is usually one person who calls the numbers. For example, a ball or chip may be labeled "B12." Players then look under the "B" column for the number 12 and if it appears on their card, they place a marker on top of it. If there isn't a 12 under the letter "B" on a player's card, then they simply wait for the next number to be called.

8.   Players then look under the "B" column for the number 12 and if it appears on his card, they place a marker on top of it.
     (Rigorous)

     A.   He

     B.   their

     C.   him

     D.   No change is necessary.

Answer: B. their
The sentence begins with the plural word "player" and is followed by the plural word "they." Therefore, the possessive word "their" is needed rather than the singular word "he" or "him."

9. **Bingo is used as a learning and entertainment tool for children.**
   (Rigorous)

   A.   Bingo is used as a learning tool and entertainment for children.

   B.   Bingo is used for learning and entertainment for children.

   C.   Bingo is used to both teach and entertain children.

   D.   No change is necessary

Answer: C. Bingo is used to both teach and entertain children.
The best answer is choice C because the correlative conjunction both is used, and there is a similar sentence structure on both sides of the word. In both choices A and B, the words being compared do not have the same structure.

10. **Players then look under the "B" column for the number 12 and if it appears on their card, they place a marker on top of it.**
    (Rigorous)

    A.   Players then look under the, "B" column for the number 12, and if it appears on their card they place a marker on top of it.

    B.   Players then look under the "B" column for the number, 12, and if it appears on their card they place a marker on top of it.

    C.   Players then look under the "B" column for the number 12 and if it appears on their card they place a marker on top of it.

    D.   No change necessary

Answer: D. No change necessary
The way that the original sentence is punctuated is the correct way to punctuate it. A comma needs to appear after "card," because it separates a dependent clause from and independent clause.

Directions: The passage below contains many errors. Read the passage. Then, answer each test item by choosing the option that corrects an error in the underlined portion(s). No more than one underlined error will appear in each item. If no error exists, choose "No change is necessary."

A family of four, consisting of two children and two adults, were trying to decide where they should go to have lunch at. Each of them wanted something different, so deciding between four places was not an easy task. The youngest child wanted fast food of course simply because they wanted to get the toy prize of the week. The eldest child was watching her weight and wanted to skip lunch altogether. The Mother was in the mood for a nice deli sandwich, one with many layers of ham and cheese. The father wanted a nice juicy burger – but not the kind from a fast food establishment. After much minutes of deliberating, the family decided to simply return home for leftover chicken from the night before.

11. The <u>youngest</u> child wanted fast <u>food of course</u> simply because they <u>wanted</u> to get the toy prize of the week.
    (Average)

    A.   young

    B.   food, of course,

    C.   want

    D.   No change is necessary

Answer: B. food, of course,
"Of course" is a clause that is added into the sentence, and therefore, requires commas on either side. The sentence could exist without the addition of the words, "of course" and therefore, needs that punctuation.

12. The youngest <u>child</u> wanted fast food of course <u>simply</u> because <u>they</u> wanted to get the toy prize of the week.
   (Average)

    A.   children

    B.   simple

    C.   she

    D.   No change is necessary

Answer: C. she
The sentence begins by drawing attention to the youngest child. Therefore, the pronoun used must agree with the singular. "She" is needed rather than "they."

13. A family of <u>four, consisting</u> of two children and two adults, were trying to <u>decide</u> where they should go to have <u>lunch at.</u>
   (Rigorous)

    A.   four consisting

    B.   deciding

    C.   lunch.

    D.   No change is necessary

Answer: C. lunch.
Sentences should not end with a preposition. The sentence should simply read, "...were trying to decide where they should go to have lunch."

14. <u>Each</u> of them wanted something different, so <u>deciding</u> <u>between</u> four places was not an easy task.
   (Rigorous)

   A.   One

   B.   decided

   C.   among

   D.   No change is necessary

Answer: C. among
In this case, you must use "among," as "between" should only be used when comparing two items.

15. After <u>much</u> minutes of deliberating, the family <u>decided</u> to <u>simply</u> return home for leftover chicken from the night before.
   (Average)

   A.   many

   B.   decides

   C.   simple

   D.   No change is necessary.

Answer: A. many
The word "many" is needed instead because the minutes could be counted as individual items as in, "How *many* minutes?" "Much" is used when an exact number cannot be determined. "How *much* detergent do I need to put in the washer?"

16. **The Mother was in the mood for a nice deli sandwich, one with many layers of ham and cheese.**
    (Easy)

    A.   The mother

    B.   much

    C.   layer

    D.   No change is necessary

Answer: A. The mother
Only when words like mom or mother are used as names, should they have a capital letter. For example, "Mom said I could wear this dress today." Mom is being used as a name and therefore requires a capital letter.

Directions: The passage below contains many errors. Read the passage. Then, answer each test item by choosing the option that corrects an error in the underlined portion(s). No more than one underlined error will appear in each item. If no error exists, choose "No change is necessary."

California is known for many things. But do you know what dates back to 1874 when the gold minors invaded California? It's the tough as old boots, Levi's denim jeans. These jeans were originally made for the minors whom needed pants to withstand the rough terrain they often encountered. Levi Straus used heavy canvas fabric and brass ribbets in the seams to withstand the test of time. Not only are these jeans more tougher than any other denim jeans on the market for they are also very fashionable.

17. **Not only are these jeans more tougher than any other denim jeans on the market for they are also very fashionable.**
    (Average)

    A.   tougher

    B.   then

    C.   market, for

    D.   No change is necessary

Answer: A. tougher
The correct form of the word "more tough" is "tougher."

BASIC SKILLS

18. <u>California</u> is known for <u>many things</u>.
   (Easy)

   A.   California, is known...

   B.   much

   C.   things!

   D.   No change is necessary

Answer: D. No change is necessary
The way this simple sentence is written is punctuated and written correctly.

19. These jeans were <u>originally</u> made for the <u>minors whom</u> needed pants
   to withstand <u>the rough terrain</u> they often encountered.
   (Rigorous)

   A.   original

   B.   miners who

   C.   the rough terrain,

   D.   No change is necessary

Answer: B. miners who
There are two errors in this section. Miners is spelled incorrectly, and the word
"whom" is only used as a pronoun when it is replacing a noun. The word "whom"
in this sentence is acting as a descriptor of the miners and therefore should be
"who."

20. **These jeans were originally made for the miners who needed pants to withstand the rough terrain they often encountered.**

    How should this sentence be rewritten?
    (Rigorous)

    A.   These jeans were originally made for the miners that needed pants to withstand the rough terrain. They often encountered.

    B.   The miners needed jeans that could withstand the rough terrain they often encountered.

    C.   These jeans were originally made for the rough terrain the miners needed.

    D.   These jeans were originally made to withstand the rough terrain that the miners often encountered.

Answer: D. These jeans were originally made to withstand the rough terrain that the miners often encountered.
In the original sentence, the pronoun "they" is not distinctly assigned and can either represent the miners or the jeans. Choice D makes the idea much clearer and assigns the pronoun to the miners.

21. **Not only are these jeans tougher than any other denim jeans on the market for they are also very fashionable.**
    (Rigorous)

    How should this sentence be rewritten?

    A.   Not only are these jeans tougher than any other denim jeans on the market, for they are also very fashionable.

    B.   Not only are these jeans tougher than any other denim jeans on the market but they are also more fashionable.

    C.   Not only are these jeans tougher than any other denim jeans on the market, but they are also very fashionable.

    D.   Not only, are these jeans tougher than any other denim jeans on the market, but, they are also very fashionable.

Answer: C. Not only are these jeans tougher than any other denim jeans on the market, but they are also very fashionable.

22. **What does the idiom "tough as old boots" mean in the sentence, "It's the tough as old boots, Levi's denim jeans."**
    (Average)

    A. Very rugged

    B. Made of leather

    C. As old as boots

    D. Worn out and old

Answer: A. Very rugged
The saying, "tough as old boots" means that they are sturdy and rugged. This expression is used to describe Levi's denim jeans.

23. **Levi Straus used heavy canvas fabric and brass ribbets in the seams to withstand the test of time.**
    (Easy)

    Which word is used incorrectly in the sentence?

    A. heavy

    B. ribbets

    C. seams

    D. time

Answer: B. ribbets
The correct word that should have been used in the sentence is "rivets."

Directions: Read the following passage and answer questions 24–32.

I can't hardly believe that Kings dominion is opening again for the season this week. This season should be much more excitable because of the introduction of the new roller coaster – the Intimidator 305. Not only is it the 15th roller coaster that the park has ejected, but it is also the tallest and most fast coaster on the East Coast. The attendees of the park are looking forward to riding the newer roller coaster, that was concluded on January 9, 2010.

24. **Not only is it the 15th roller coaster that the park has erected, but it is also the <u>tallest</u> and <u>most fast</u> coaster on the <u>East Coast.</u>**
    (Easy)

    A.   taller

    B.   fastest

    C.   East coast

    D.   No change is necessary

Answer: B. fastest
The two adjectives must agree, and the adjective tallest is used first. Therefore, the comparative adjective to use would be fastest.

25. **The <u>attendees</u> of the park <u>are</u> looking forward to riding the <u>newer</u> roller coaster, that was concluded on January 9, 2010.**
    (Average)

    A.   attendance

    B.   were

    C.   newest

    D.   No change is necessary

Answer: C. newest
"Newer" could be used if only two items were being compared. However, the passage states that this is the 15th roller coaster that has been added. Therefore, "newest" would be the correct word to use.

26. **The season <u>should be</u> <u>much more</u> <u>excitable</u> because of the introduction of the new roller coaster.**
(Average)

      A.   shouldn't be

      B.   more

      C.   exciting

      D.   No change is necessary

Answer: C. exciting
"Excitable" is the wrong adjective needed to describe the new season. It should be much more exciting.

27. **The attendees of the park are <u>looking</u> forward to riding the newest roller coaster that was <u>concluded</u> on <u>January 9, 2010.</u>**
(Average)

      A.   looked

      B.   completed

      C.   January 9 2010

      D.   No change is necessary

Answer: B. completed
"Concluded" is used with an idea. For example, the jury concluded that the defendant was guilty. When being used with an object, like a roller coaster, then the word completed is used.

28. I **can't hardly** believe that **Kings** dominion is opening again for the season this **week**.
(Easy)

   A.   can

   B.   King's

   C.   weekly

   D.   No change is necessary

Answer: A. can
The way the sentence is written now, "I can't hardly believe," it contains a double negative. The correct way to say that is, "I can hardly believe..."

29. **Not only** is it the 15th roller coaster that the park has **ejected**, but it is also the **tallest** and most fast coaster on the East Coast.
(Rigorous)

   A.   Not only,

   B.   erected

   C.   taller

   D.   No change is necessary

Answer: B. erected
"Ejected" means to force something out. Erect means to put something upright (like a roller coaster). The wrong word was written in the paragraph.

30. **This season should be much more excitable because of the introduction of the <u>new roller coaster—the Intimidator 305.</u>**
(Rigorous)

   A.   the new roller coaster, the Intimidator 305.

   B.   the new roller coaster – the Intimidator 305?

   C.   the new, roller coaster, the Intimidator 305.

   D.   No change is necessary

Answer: D. No change is necessary
There is no change necessary. A dash or hyphen is an acceptable form of punctuation, and this is a great way to use one.

31. **The attendees of the park are looking forward to riding the newest <u>roller coaster, that</u> was concluded on January 9, 2010.**
(Rigorous)

   A.   roller, coaster that

   B.   roller coaster that,

   C.   roller coaster that

   D.   No change is necessary

Answer: C. roller coaster that
No comma is needed between roller coaster and that because there are two independent clauses being joined.

32. **I can hardly believe that <u>Kings dominion</u> is opening again for the season this week.**
(Average)

   A.   King's dominion

   B.   Kings Dominion

   C.   kings dominion

   D.   No change is necessary

Answer: B. King Dominion
Kings Dominion is the proper name of an amusement park. Therefore, both names must be capitalized.

Directions: Read the following passage and answer questions 33–38.

It is a requirement that all parents volunteer two hours during the course of the season. Or an alternative was to pay $8 so you can have some high school students work a shift for you. Lots of parents liked this idea and will take advantage of the opportunity. Shifts run an hour long, and it is well worth it to pay the money so you don't miss your sons game.

33. **It is a requirement that all parents volunteer two hours during the course of the season.**
   (Average)

   How should the above sentence be rewritten?

   A.   It is a requirement of all parents volunteering two hours during the course of the season.

   B.   It is required of all parents to volunteer for two hours during the course of the season.

   C.   They require all parents volunteer during the season.

   D.   Requiring all parents to volunteer for two hours over the course of the season.

Answer: B. It is required of all parents to volunteer for two hours during the course of the season.
This is the only choice that will work. Choice C makes sense, but the pronoun "they" is not established and cannot be used in the first sentence of the paragraph.

34. **An alternative <u>was</u> to pay $8 so you can have some <u>high school</u> students work a shift for you.**
   (Average)

   A.   is

   B.   High School

   C.   High school

   D.   No change is necessary.

Answer: A. is
The first sentence puts this passage in the present tense. Therefore, the verb tense must remain the same throughout the passage and "was" is a past tense verb.

35. Many parents liked this idea and will take advantage of the opportunity.

How should the sentence be rewritten?
(Rigorous)

A.   Many parent's liked this idea and took advantage of the opportunity.

B.   Many parents like this idea and take advantage of the opportunity.

C.   Many parents like this idea and took advantage of the opportunity.

D.   Many parents did like this idea and take advantage of the opportunity.

Answer: B. Many parents like this idea and take advantage of the opportunity.
The verb tense between "like" and "take" must remain consistent in the sentence and consistent with the verb tense of the paragraph.

36. Shifts run an hour long, and it is well worth it to pay the money so you don't miss your sons games.
(Average)

A.   Shift's

B.   too

C.   son's

D.   No change is necessary

Answer: C. son's
"Son's game" is possessive. Therefore, an apostrophe is needed to show possession.

37. **It is a requirement that all <u>parents</u> volunteer two <u>hours</u> during the course of the season.**
   (Easy)

   A.   parent's

   B.   parents'

   C.   hour's

   D.   No change is necessary

Answer: D. No change is necessary
This sentence is grammatically and mechanically correct. No change is needed. Apostrophes are only used to show possession or contractions. The words used in the sentence are simply plural nouns and do not show possession.

38. **<u>Or an</u> alternative was to pay $8 so you can have some <u>high school students</u> work a shift for you.**
   (Rigorous)

   A.   An

   B.   high-school

   C.   student's

   D.   No change is necessary

Answer: A. An
"Or" is not needed to begin this sentence. The conjunction "or" should be used to join two clauses without the use of a period.

BASIC SKILLS

Answer Key: Writing

1.	A		20.	D
2.	C		21.	C
3.	B		22.	A
4.	A		23.	B
5.	A		24.	B
6.	B		25.	C
7.	A		26.	C
8.	B		27.	B
9.	C		28.	A
10.	D		29.	B
11.	B		30.	D
12.	C		31.	C
13.	C		32.	B
14.	C		33.	B
15.	A		34.	A
16.	A		35.	B
17.	A		36.	C
18.	D		37.	D
19.	B		38.	A

Rigor Table: Writing

	Easy 21%	Average 39.5%	Rigorous 39.5%
Questions	2, 4, 16, 18, 23, 24, 28, 37	1, 5, 7, 11, 12, 15, 17, 22, 25, 26, 27, 32, 33, 34, 36	3, 6, 8, 9, 10, 13, 14, 19, 20, 21, 29, 30, 31, 35, 38

Writing Essay

Although the marvels of technology surround us every day, there are moments when we all would give anything to be freed from that technology.

Discuss the extent to which you agree or disagree with this opinion. Support your views with specific reasons and examples from your own experience, observations, or reading.

Sample Good Response

Although technology has made our lives much easier, it has also made our lives more complicated and eaten into our free time and family time. Technology has made it possible to track our children with GPS in cell phones, and it has made our cars easier to navigate and safer to drive. It has also given us access to a world of knowledge by placing the Internet at our fingertips. However, it has also impeded on our personal lives and in some instances made us slaves to its ease, and there are moments when we all would give anything to be freed from that technology.

With the increase of technology it seems as if we are never able to leave work behind. Even though we may leave our offices or our classrooms at the end of the day, we are still connected through technology and email. There are too many of us who, although we are home and should be more connected with our families, often check their email. I myself am guilty of this act. Although I have left school at the end of the day, each evening I check my school email account even though it isn't necessary. We are too connected to technology and feel that we need to stay on top of it at all times of the day.

Not only do people feel the need to check their work email accounts nightly, with the introduction of Blackberries and text messaging, we now stay connected no matter where we are. Too many people "take a vacation" but don't really take a vacation. Even while we are officially away from work and are "on vacation," we continue to check our email either via computer or via phone. We find it a necessity to stay connected at all times. I too am guilty of this act and always check my email using my cell phone even when I don't have a computer available. Again, it would be great to be freed from the marvel of technology that surrounds us daily.

There have been a few times where I have ignored the phone and ignored email, and have even not watched the news on television for a few days and took an official vacation—and it felt liberating. I felt very free and rejuvenated. Our culture should take a true vacation more often from technology. It is certainly a lot cheaper than going to an expensive spa to rejuvenate the soul and certainly will have a longer lasting effect.

BASIC SKILLS

Sample Poor Response

We should all take a vacation from technology. We have become too dependent upon it. We carry phones, have email, and are attached to the Internet 24/7. We are slaves to technology.

I check my email every night even though I have left the office. I feel the need to constantly be connected to everyone. Many people check their email through Blackberries and other cell phones. I often do that and would love to not feel it necessary to check my email through my phone. I would love to take a break or a vacation.

Technology isn't just email, however. We need to remove ourselves from the media and the Internet too.

MATH

1. **Which of the following is correct?**
    (Easy)

    A.   2365 > 2340

    B.   0.75 > 1.25

    C.   3/4 < 1/16

    D.   -5 < -6

Answer: A. 2365 > 2340

2. **Simplify:**

    $$\frac{5^{-2} \times 5^3}{5^5 \times 5^{-7}}$$

    (Average)

    A. 5^5

    B.   125

    C. $\dfrac{1}{125}$

    D.   25

Answer: B. 125

$$\frac{5^{-2} \times 5^3}{5^5 \times 5^{-7}} = \frac{5^{-2+3}}{5^{5-7}} = \frac{5}{5^{-2}} = 5^{1+2} = 5^3 = 125$$

3. Choose the set in which the members are <u>not</u> equivalent.
   (Average)

   A.   1/2, 0.5, 50%

   B.   10/5, 2.0, 200%

   C.   3/8, 0.385, 38.5%

   D.   7/10, 0.7, 70%

Answer: C. 3/8, 0.385, 38.5%

3/8 is equivalent to .375 and 37.5%.

4. The digit 8 in the number 975.086 is in the
   (Easy)

   A.   Tenths place

   B.   Ones place

   C.   Hundredths place

   D.   Hundreds place

Answer: C. Hundredths place

5. The relations given below demonstrate the following addition and multiplication property of real numbers:

a + b = b + a

ab = ba

(Easy)

A.   Commutative

B.   Associative

C.   Identity

D.   Inverse

Answer: A. Commutative

Both addition and multiplication of real numbers satisfy the commutative property according to which changing the order of the operands does not change the result of the operation.

6. **Simplify:**

$$\frac{27 - 2.3^2}{8 \div 2^2 - (-2)^2}$$

(Rigorous)

A.   9/2

B.   9/8

C.   -4.5

D.   0.75

Answer is C. -4.5

Following the order of operations: $\dfrac{27 - 2.3^2}{8 \div 2^2 - (-2)^2} = \dfrac{27 - 18}{2 - 4} = -\dfrac{9}{2} = -4.5$

7.   At a publishing company, Mona can proofread 300 pages in 5 hours while Lisa can proofread 360 pages in 4 hours. If they share the task of proofreading a 375 page document, how long will it take them to complete the job?
     (Rigorous)

     A.   2.5 hours

     B.   5 hours

     C.   3 hours

     D.   3.5 hours

Answer: A. 2.5 hours
Since Mona proofreads 300/5 = 60 pages in one hour and Lisa proofreads 360/4 = 90 pages in one hour, together they can proofread 90 + 60 = 150 pages per hour. Hence, it would take then 375/150 = 2.5 hours to complete the job.

8.   A student had 60 days to appeal the results of an exam. If the results were received on March 23, what was the last day that the student could appeal?
     (Average)

     A.   May 21

     B.   May 22

     C.   May 23

     D.   May 24

Answer: B. May 22
Recall that there are 30 days in April and 31 in March. 8 days in March + 30 days in April + 22 days in May brings him to a total of 60 days on May 22.

9. **A coat is on sale for $135. If the discount offered is 25%, what was the original price of the coat?**
(Rigorous)

   A. $160

   B. $180

   C. $110

   D. $150

Answer: B. $180
Since the discount is 25%, the sale price $135 is 75% of the original price. Hence

$$\frac{135}{75} \times \frac{100}{1} = \frac{540}{3} = \$180$$

10. **If three cups of concentrate are needed to make 2 gallons of fruit punch, how many cups are needed to make 5 gallons?**
(Average)

   A.   6 cups

   B.   7 cups

   C.   7.5 cups

   D.   10 cups

Answer: C. 7.5 cups
Set up the proportion 3/2 = x/5, cross multiply to obtain 15=2x, then divide both sides by 2.

11. **A sofa sells for $520. If the retailer makes a 30% profit, what was the wholesale price?**
   (Average)

   A.   400

   B. $676

   C. $490

   D. $364

Answer: A. $400
Let x be the wholesale price; then x + .30x = 520, 1.30x = 520. Divide both sides by 1.30.

12. **What is the negation of a statement of the form "p and q"?**
   (Average)

   A.   not and not q

   B.   not p and q

   C.   not p or not q

   D.   p or not q

Answer: C. not p or not q

13. **The contrapositive of the statement "If I am hungry I eat" is:**
   (Average)

   A.   If I eat then I am hungry

   B.   If I am not hungry I do not eat

   C.   If I do not eat I am not hungry

   D.   None of the above

Answer: C. If I do not eat I am not hungry
The contrapositive of the statement "if p then q" is given by "if not q then not p."

14. **Solve for x:**

$3(5 + 3x) - 8 = 88$

(Average)

    A.   30

    B.   9

    C.   4.5

    D.   27

Answer is B. 9
$3(5 + 3x) - 8 = 88$; $15 + 9x - 8 = 88$; $7 + 9x = 88$; $9x = 81$; $x = 9$

15. **Solve for x:**

$|2x + 3| > 4$

(Rigorous)

    A. $-\frac{7}{2} > x > \frac{1}{2}$

    B. $-\frac{1}{2} > x > \frac{7}{2}$

    C. $x < \frac{7}{2}$ or $x < -\frac{1}{2}$

    D. $x < -\frac{7}{2}$ or $x > \frac{1}{2}$

Answer: D. $x < -\frac{7}{2}$ or $x > \frac{1}{2}$
The quantity within the absolute value symbols must be either > 4 or < -4. Solve the two inequalities $2x + 3 > 4$ or $2x + 3 < -4$

16. You are helping students list the steps needed to solve the word problem:

"Mr. Jones is 5 times as old as his son. Two years later he will be 4 times as old as his son. How old is Mr. Jones?"

One of the students makes the following list:

1.　　Assume Mr. Jones' son is x years old. Express Mr. Jones' age in terms of x.
2.　　Write how old they will be two years later in terms of x.
3.　　Solve the equation for x.
4.　　Multiply the answer by 5 to get Mr. Jones' age.

What step is missing between steps 2 and 3?
(Rigorous)

A.　　Write an equation setting Mr. Jones age equal to 5 times his son's age

B.　　Write an equation setting Mr. Jones age two years later equal to 5 times his son's age two years later

C.　　Write an equation setting Mr. Jones age equal to 4 times his son's age

D.　　Write an equation setting Mr. Jones age two years later equal to 4 times his son's age two years later

Answer: D. Write an equation setting Mr. Jones age two years later equal to 4 times his son's age two years later

17. **The following equation is the best choice for teaching use of the distributive law in solving equations:**
    (Rigorous)

    A. $3(x + 5) = 4x$

    B. $x(3 + 5) = 4$

    C. $4(x + 2x) = 2$

    D.   None of the above

Answer is A. $3(x + 5) = 4x$
One can apply the distributive law to choice B, but it is simpler to just add 3 and 5 and then multiply by x. One can also apply the distributive law to choice C, but the simpler option is to add x and 2x first and then multiply by 4. To solve choice A, one would have to apply the distributive law $3(x + 5) = 3x + 15$. Hence, A is the best choice.

18. **What is the next term in the sequence**

    0.005, 0.03, 0.18, 1.08...

    (Rigorous)

    A.   1.96

    B.   2.16

    C.   3.32

    D.   6.48

Answer is D. 6.48
This is a geometric sequence where each term is obtained by multiplying the preceding term by the common ration 6. Thus, the next term in the sequence is 1.08 x 6 = 6.48.

19. {1,4,7,10, . . .}

What is the 40th term in this sequence?
(Average)

    A.   43

    B.   121

    C.   118

    D.   120

Answer: C. 118
This is an arithmetic sequence with first term 1 and common difference 3. Hence, the 40th term is $1 + (40 - 1)3 = 1 + 39 \times 3 = 1 + 117 = 118$.

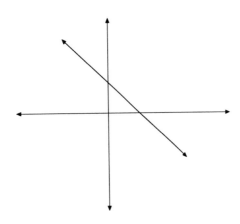

20. Which equation is represented by the above graph?
(Average)

    A. $x - y = 3$

    B. $x - y = -3$

    C. $x + y = 3$

    D. $x + y = -3$

Answer: C. x + y = 3
By looking at the graph, we can determine the slope to be −1 and the y-intercept to be 3. Write the slope intercept form of the line as $y = -1x + 3$. Add x to both sides to obtain $x + y = 3$, the equation in standard form.

21. Graph the solution:

$|x| + 7 < 13$

(Average)

A)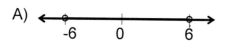

B)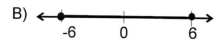

C)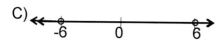

D)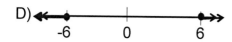

Answer: A.
Solve by adding -7 to each side of the inequality. Since the absolute value of x is less than 6, x must be between -6 and 6. The end points are not included so the circles on the graph are hollow.

22. Which of the following shapes is not a parallelogram?
   (Easy)

I

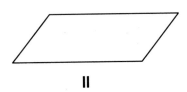

II

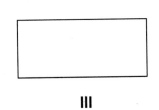

III

A.   I & III

B.   II & III

C.   I

D.   I, II & III

Answer is C. I
A parallelogram is a quadrilateral with two pairs of parallel sides.

23. **An isosceles triangle has:**
    (Easy)

    A.   Three equal sides

    B.   Two equal sides

    C.   No equal sides

    D.   Two equal sides in some cases, no equal sides in others

Answer: B. Two equal sides

24. **Given similar polygons with corresponding sides of lengths 9 and 15, find the perimeter of the smaller polygon if the perimeter of the larger polygon is 150 units.**
    (Rigorous)

    A.   54

    B.   135

    C.   90

    D.   126

Answer: C. 90
The perimeters of similar polygons are directly proportional to the lengths of their sides, therefore 9/15 = x/150. Cross multiply to obtain 1350 = 15x, then divide by 15 to obtain the perimeter of the smaller polygon.

25. Ginny and Nick head back to their respective colleges after being home for the weekend. They leave their house at the same time and drive for 4 hours. Ginny drives due south at the average rate of 60 miles per hour, and Nick drives due east at the average rate of 60 miles per hour. What is the straight-line distance between them, in miles, at the end of the 4 hours?
(Rigorous)

A. $120\sqrt{2}$

B. 240

C. $240\sqrt{2}$

D. 288

Answer: C. $240\sqrt{2}$
Draw a picture.

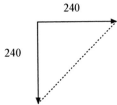

We have a right triangle, so we can use the Pythagorean Theorem to find the distance between the two points.

$$240^2 + 240^2 = c^2$$

$$2(240)^2 = c^2$$

$$240\sqrt{2} = c$$

26. Given segment AC with B as its midpoint find the coordinates of C if A = (5,7) and B = (3, 6.5).
    (Rigorous)

    A.   (4, 6.5)

    B.   (1, 6)

    C.   (2, 0.5)

    D.   (16, 1)

Answer: B. (1, 6)
Let (x,y) be the coordinates of C. Using the midpoint formula, the coordinates of B can be expressed as follows:

3 = (5+x)/2 ; 6.5 = (7 + y)/2

Solving for x and y we get, x = 1 and y = 6.

27. The following set of points on a coordinate plane define an isosceles right triangle
    (Rigorous)

    A.   (4,0), (0,4), (4,4)

    B.   (4,0), (0,6), (4,4)

    C.   (0,0), (0,4), (5,2)

    D.   (0,0), (5.0), (5,2)

Answer: A. (4,0), (0,4), (4,4)
Choice D defines a right triangle that is not isosceles, choice C defines an isosceles triangle that is not right, and choice B defines a triangle that is neither isosceles nor right.

28. The speed of light in space is about 3×10^8 meters per second. Express this in Kilometers per hour.
(Average)

    A. 1.08×10^9 Km / hr

    B. 3.0×10^{11} Km / hr

    C. 1.08×10^{12} Km / hr

    D. 1.08×10^{15} Km / hr

Answer: A. 1.08×10^9 Km / hr

$$3 \times 10^8 \, \frac{m}{s} = 3 \times 10^8 \, \frac{m}{s} \times \frac{1 Km}{1000m} \times \frac{3600s}{1\,hr} = 108 \times 10^7 \, \frac{Km}{hr} = 1.08 \times 10^9 \, \frac{Km}{hr}$$

29. Given a 30 meter x 60 meter garden with a circular fountain with a 5 meter radius, calculate the area of the portion of the garden not occupied by the fountain.
(Rigorous)

    A.   1721 m²

    B.   1879 m²

    C.   2585 m²

    D.   1015 m²

Answer: A. 1721 m²
Find the area of the garden and then subtract the area of the fountain: 30(60)– $\pi(5)^2$, or approximately 1721 square meters

30. **What is the length of a fourth of the circumference of a circle with a diameter of 24 cm?**
    (Rigorous)

    A.   18.85

    B.   75.4

    C.   32.45

    D.   20.75

Answer: A. 18.85
The circumference of the circle is πd, where d is 24. Π(24)= 75.4; one fourth of that is 18.85.

31. **What percentage of students got a C grade?**
    (Average)

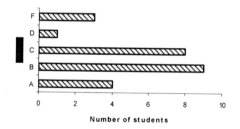

Number of students

    A.   35

    B.   8

    C.   32

    D.   40

Answer: C. 32
The total number of students = 4 + 9 + 8 + 1 + 3 = 25. The number of students who got C = 8. Hence, the percentage of students that got C = (8/25)x100= 32.

32. **Which statement is true about George's budget?**
    (Easy)

   A.   George spends the greatest portion of his income on food

   B.   George spends twice as much on utilities as he does on his mortgage

   C.   George spends twice as much on utilities as he does on food

   D.   George spends the same amount on food and utilities as he does on mortgage

Answer: C. George spends twice as much on utilities as he does on food

33. **You are creating a pie chart to show the expenses for a business. If employee pay is 40% of the total expenditure, what central angle will you use to show that segment of the pie chart?**
    (Average)

   A. 72°

   B. 80°

   C. 40°

   D. 144°

Answer: D. 144°
Since employee pay is 40% of the total, the central angle will be 40% of 360° = $(40/100) \times 360^\circ = 144^\circ$.

34. **Which of the following is the most accurate inference that can be made from the graph shown below?**
(Average)

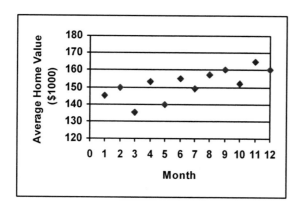

A.   The average home value shows a decreasing trend over the 12-month period

B.   The average home value shows an increasing trend over the 12-month period

C.   The average home value stays about the same over the 12-month period

D.   The data fluctuates too much to make any comment about the trend

Answer: B. The average home value shows an increasing trend over the 12-month period
Even though the data fluctuates, it shows an unmistakable upward trend towards the right.

35. **Melissa scores 60, 68, and 75 in the first three of five tests. What should her average score be for the last two tests so that her mean test score for the 5 tests is 70?**
    (Rigorous)

    A.   70

    B.   73.5

    C.   75.5

    D.   85

Answer: B. 73.5
Let Melissa's average score for the last two tests be x. Then,
$60 + 68 + 75 + 2x = 70 \times 5$
$2x = 350 - 203 = 147$
$x = 73.5$

36. **Find the median of the following set of data:**

    14 3 7 6 11 20

    (Easy)

    A.   9

    B.   8.5

    C.   7

    D.   11

Answer: A. 9
Place the numbers is ascending order: 3 6 7 11 14 20. Find the average of the middle two numbers (7+11)/2 =9.

37. **Corporate salaries are listed for several employees. Which would be the best measure of central tendency?**
    (Average)

    $24,000 $24,000 $26,000
    $28,000 $30,000 $120,000

    A.   Mean

    B.   Median

    C.   Mode

    D.   No difference

Answer: B. median
The median provides the best measure of central tendency, in this case where the mode is the lowest number and the mean would be disproportionately skewed by the outlier $120,000.

38. **A jar contains 3 red marbles, 5 white marbles, 1 green marble and 15 blue marbles. If one marble is picked at random from the jar, what is the probability that it will be red?**
    (Easy)

    A. $\dfrac{1}{3}$

    B. $\dfrac{1}{8}$

    C. $\dfrac{3}{8}$

    D. $\dfrac{1}{24}$

Answer: B. $\dfrac{1}{8}$

The total number of marbles is 24 and the number of red marbles is 3. Thus, the probability of picking a red marble from the jar is 3/24=1/8.

39. Given a drawer with 5 black socks, 3 blue socks, and 2 red socks, what is the probability that you will draw two black socks in two draws in a dark room?
    (*Rigorous*)

    A.   2/9

    B.   1/4

    C.   17/18

    D.   1/18

Answer: A. 2/9
In this example of conditional probability, the probability of drawing a black sock on the first draw is 5/10. It is implied in the problem that there is no replacement, therefore the probability of obtaining a black sock in the second draw is 4/9. Multiply the two probabilities and reduce to lowest terms.

40. A sack of candy has 3 peppermints, 2 butterscotch drops and 3 cinnamon drops. One candy is drawn and replaced, then another candy is drawn; what is the probability that both will be butterscotch?
    (*Rigorous*)

    A.   1/2

    B.   1/28

    C.   1/4

    D.   1/16

Answer: D. 1/16
With replacement, the probability of obtaining a butterscotch on the first draw is 2/8 and the probability of drawing a butterscotch on the second draw is also 2/8. Multiply and reduce to lowest terms.

Answer Key: Mathematics

1.	A	21.	A
2.	B	22.	C
3.	C	23.	B
4.	C	24.	C
5.	A	25.	C
6.	C	26.	B
7.	A	27.	A
8.	B	28.	A
9.	B	29.	A
10.	C	30.	A
11.	A	31.	C
12.	C	32.	C
13.	C	33.	D
14.	B	34.	B
15.	D	35.	B
16.	D	36.	A
17.	A	37.	B
18.	D	38.	B
19.	C	39.	A
20.	C	40.	D

Rigor Table: Mathematics

	Easy 20%	Average 40%	Rigorous 40%
Questions	1, 4, 5, 22, 23, 32, 36, 38	2, 3, 8, 10, 11, 12, 13, 14, 19, 20, 21, 28, 31, 33, 34, 37	6, 7, 9, 15, 16, 17, 18, 24, 25, 26, 27, 29, 30, 35, 39, 40

CPSIA information can be obtained at www.ICGtesting.com
229644LV00001B/70/P